Fun at School

Written by Tracey Reeder   Photographed by Dean Iversen

Here are the children.
They are running.

Here are the children.
They are jumping.

Here are the children.

They are skipping rope.

Here are the children.
They are hopping.

Here are the children.
They are swinging.

Here are the children.
They are climbing.

Here are the children.

They are reading.